Maze Golf

The Maze Game that Scores Like Golf!
Fun *Fore* the Whole Family

By David Schneiderman

Published by
Tallfellow Press, Inc.
1180 South Beverly Drive
Los Angeles, CA 90035

Distributed to the trade by
Andrews McMeel Distribution Services
4520 Main Street
Kansas City, Missouri 64111

Cover design and production by SunDried Penguin.

ISBN 0-9676061-1-X

Printed in the USA by
10 9 8 7 6 5 4 3 2 1

Tallfellow Press
Los Angeles

INTRODUCTION

It was a surprise to everyone, including me, when my fourth grade doodles began to look like mazes. Simple ones at first, then more complex. I didn't know where this strange ability came from, I only knew that I had it, and enjoyed it. The mazes drew lots of attention and suddenly my classmates started asking me to create special ones for them. In time those mazes took on themes: finding swords to slay dragons, avoiding trolls, going through wormholes in space, etc.

Twenty years later I demonstrated this skill to a friend and—as good fortune would have it—he worked in publishing. Before I knew it, I had melded my talent with one of my passions, GOLF, and the results lie before you.

David Schneiderman

This book is dedicated to
Mom, Dad, Maggie, Steve, Rob, Joyce,
Laura and Dan...

But mostly to my wife, Tia,
whose love and support make
my dreams become realities.

PLAYING AROUND

The *objective* of **Maze Golf**, like real golf, is to get the *lowest score possible*. Playing is fun and easy. Just follow the simple instructions below.

Start each maze at the **Tee** and carefully make your way to the **Green** where you earn your score. For each **Hazard** you encounter, you must *add the appropriate amount of strokes to your score.*

As you move through the maze you will have to make choices about which route to take. Choosing a new path is like selecting the right golf club; pick wisely, your score will depend on it. You must keep going forward *(you may not go back)* and continue until you reach the green.

Scoring is simple. All scores are based on the listed **"Par"** for each hole. Par is the average score and you're trying to get as close to, or under, that number. Each **Scoring Term** has a particular relationship to the par. It works as follows:

HOLE IN ONE = **1**

EAGLE = **2 below par**   BIRDIE = **1 below par**

BOGIE = **1 above par**   +2 (or Double Bogie) = **2 above par**

Each hole has a **Legend** that will help you figure out your score. If you go **Out of Bounds (OB),** or end up in a **Water Hazard (WH),** you must *add 2 to your score* for that hole and then follow the arrow back into the maze.

And let's not forget those pesky **Sand Traps.** (Do not stop if you enter a trap. There is an exit to continue back into the maze.) For each Sand Trap you go through you must *add 1 to your score* for that hole.

It is possible to go through more than one hazard per hole, so move carefully.

Each page has a place to record your score, and there is a **Scorecard** at the end of the book. Enter your scores on the Scorecard and add them up when you're finished. You can play alone against the "par" or against an opponent.

The PAR for this course is 72.

There are two sets of mazes in this book, either play against a friend or try to beat your first score on a second round.

Good Luck!

SCORECARD

Maze Craze Country Club

HOLE	1	2	3	4	5	6	7	8	9	10	11	12	13	14	15	16	17	18	
YARDAGE	435	165	515	430	185	412	398	410	523	425	401	509	179	531	417	389	142	420	6889
PAR	4	3	5	4	3	4	4	4	5	4	4	5	3	5	4	4	3	4	72
PLAYER																			
1.																			

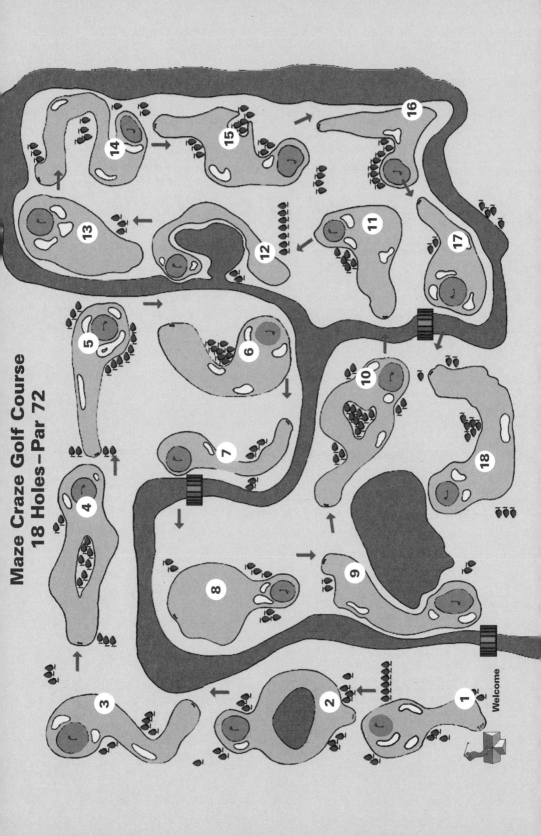

Maze Craze Golf Course
18 Holes – Par 72

Welcome

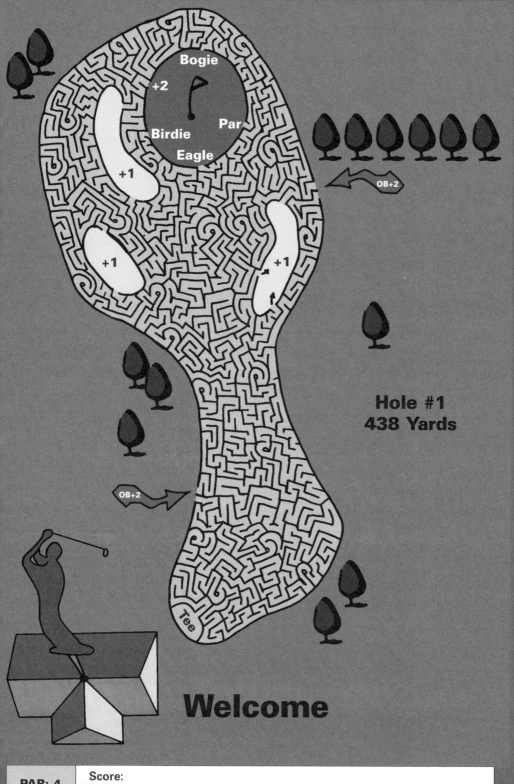

Bogie

+2

Par

Birdie

Eagle

+1

+1

+1

OB+2

OB+2

Hole #1
438 Yards

Tee

Welcome

PAR: 4	Score:			
	Eagle: 2	Birdie: 3	Bogie: 5	Double Bogie: 6

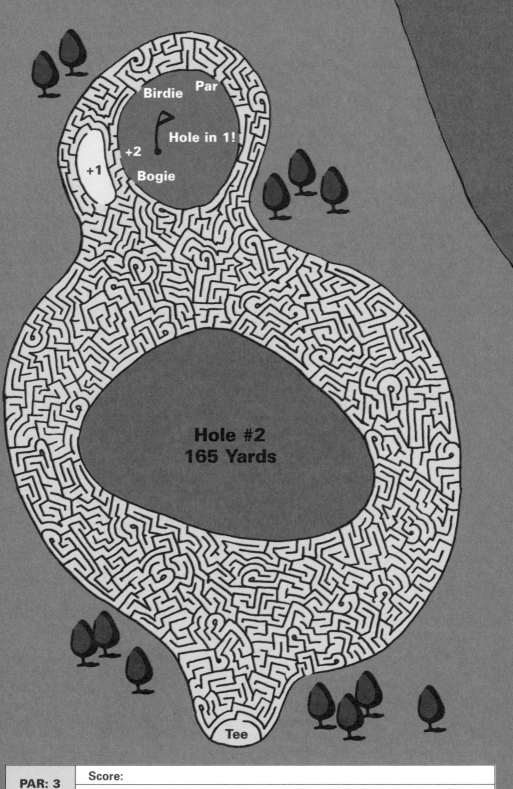

Birdie

Par

Hole in 1!

+2

+1

Bogie

Hole #2
165 Yards

Tee

PAR: 3	Score:			
	Hole in 1!: 1	Birdie: 2	Bogie: 4	Double Bogie: 5

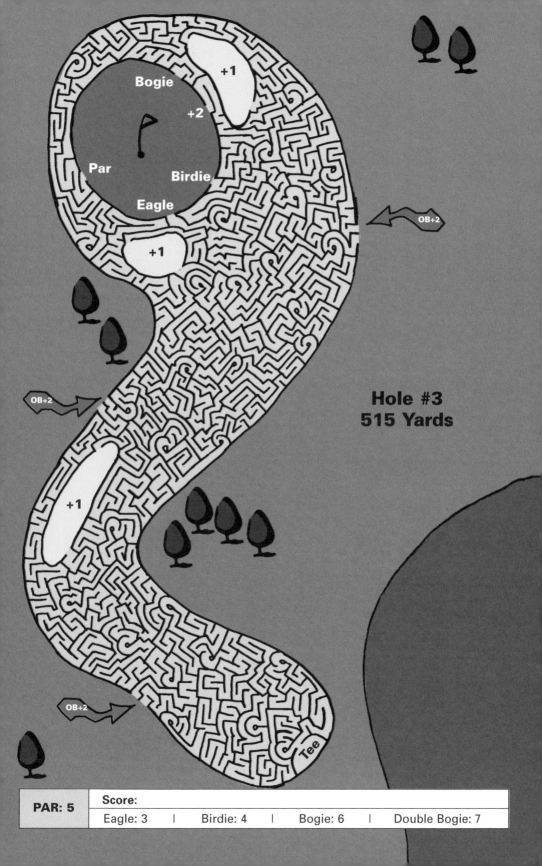

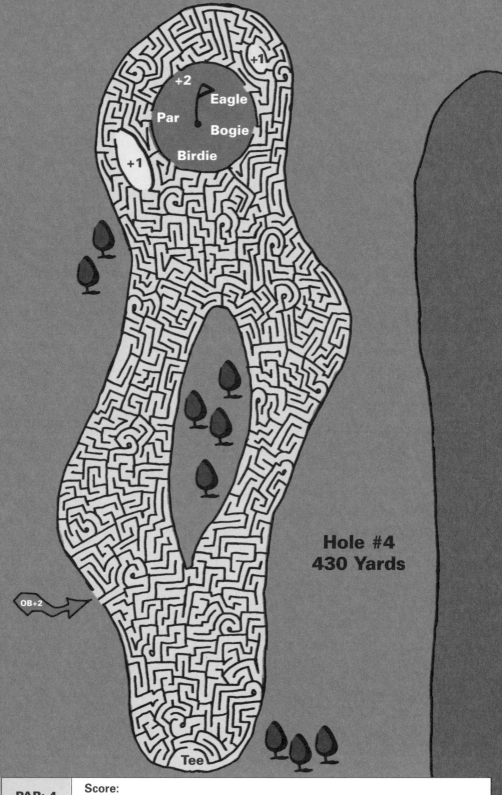

+1

+2

Eagle

Par

Bogie

Birdie

+1

OB+2

Hole #4
430 Yards

Tee

PAR: 4	Score:			
	Eagle: 2	Birdie: 3	Bogie: 5	Double Bogie: 6

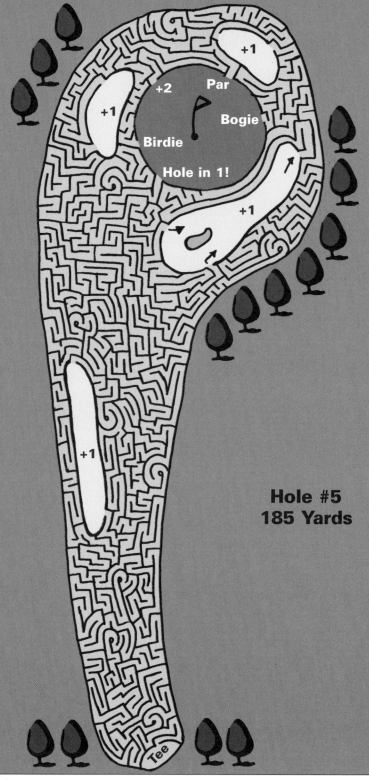

Hole #5
185 Yards

+1

+2   Par

+1   Bogie

Birdie

Hole in 1!

+1

+1

Tee

PAR: 3	Score:			
	Hole in 1!: 1	Birdie: 2	Bogie: 4	Double Bogie: 5			

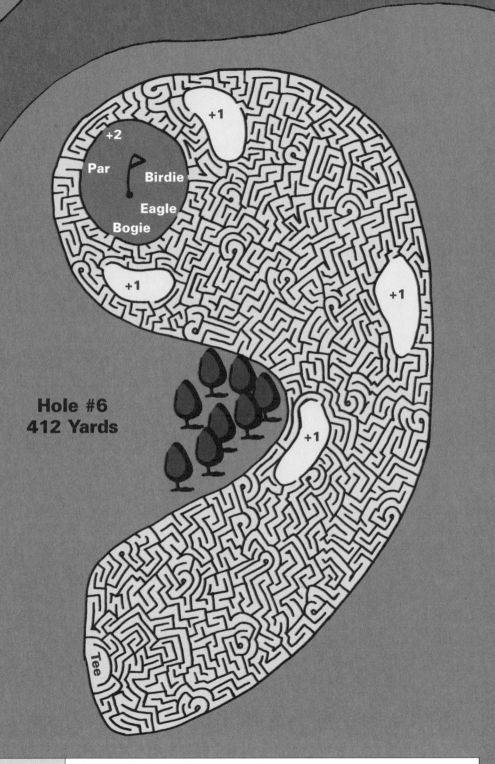

Hole #6
412 Yards

+2
Par
Birdie
Eagle
Bogie

+1

+1

+1

+1

Tee

PAR: 4	Score:			
	Eagle: 2	Birdie: 3	Bogie: 5	Double Bogie: 6

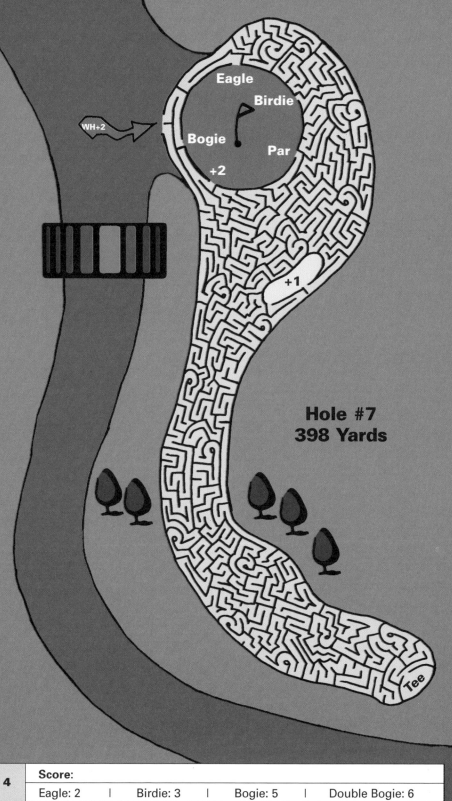

Eagle

Birdie

Bogie

Par

+2

WH+2

+1

Hole #7
398 Yards

Tee

PAR: 4	Score:			
	Eagle: 2	Birdie: 3	Bogie: 5	Double Bogie: 6

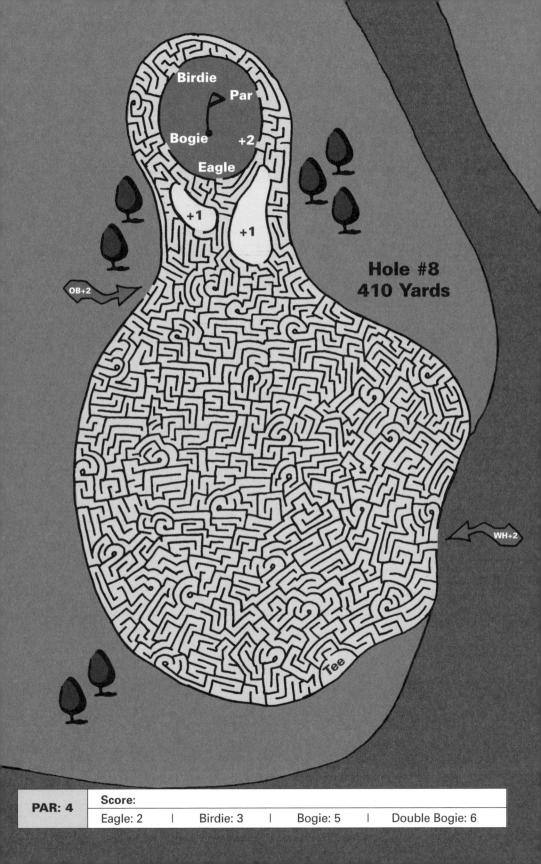

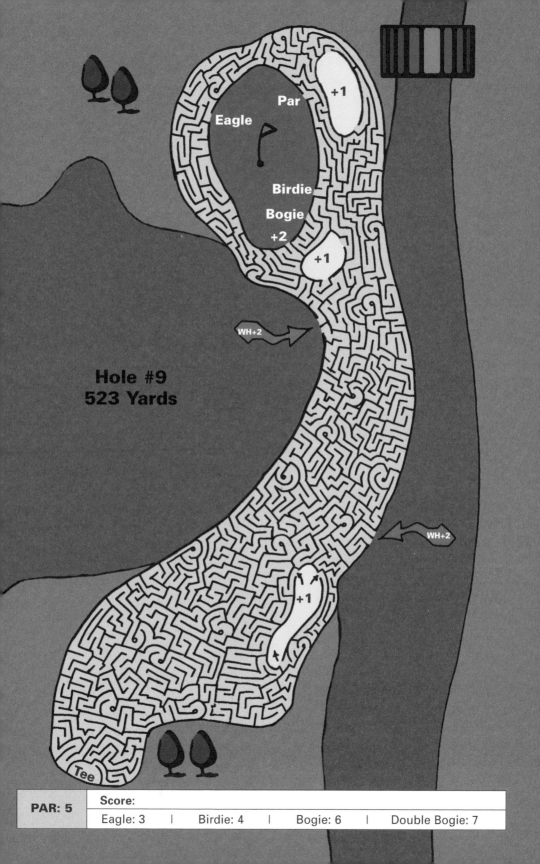

Par

Eagle

+1

Birdie

Bogie

+2

+1

WH+2

Hole #9
523 Yards

WH+2

+1

Tee

PAR: 5	Score:			
	Eagle: 3	Birdie: 4	Bogie: 6	Double Bogie: 7

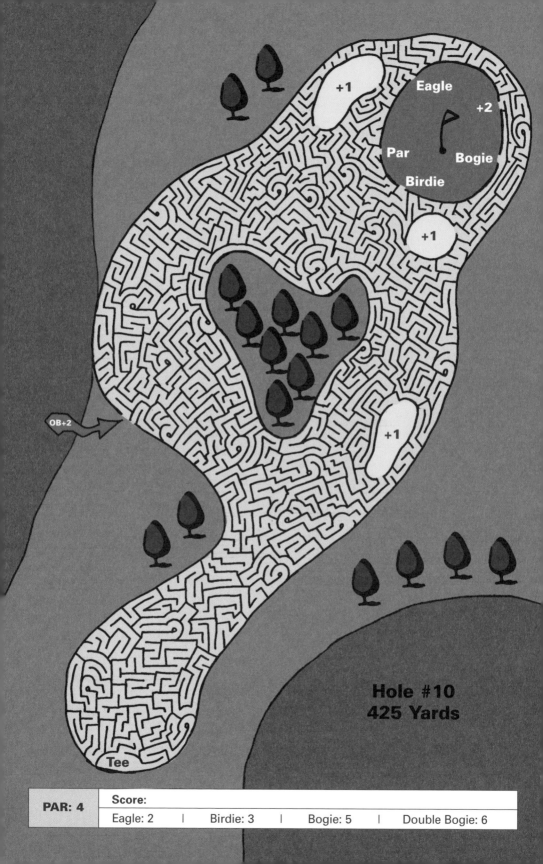

+1

Eagle

+2

Par

Bogie

Birdie

+1

OB+2

+1

Hole #10
425 Yards

Tee

PAR: 4	Score:			
	Eagle: 2	Birdie: 3	Bogie: 5	Double Bogie: 6

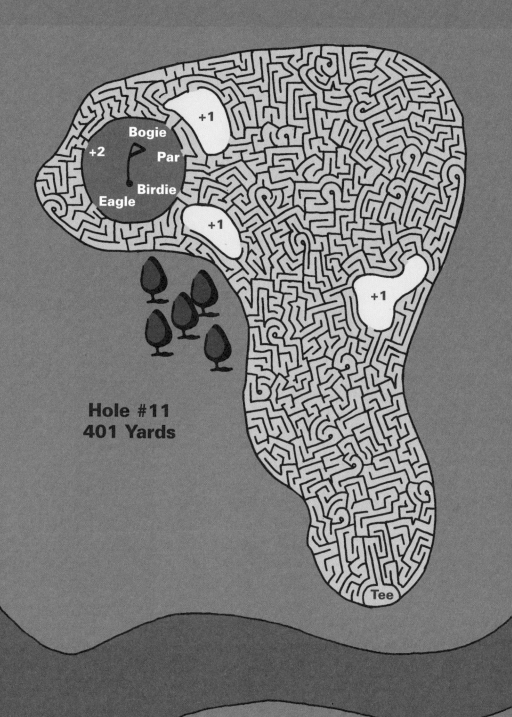

Hole #11
401 Yards

PAR: 4	Score:			
	Eagle: 2	Birdie: 3	Bogie: 5	Double Bogie: 6

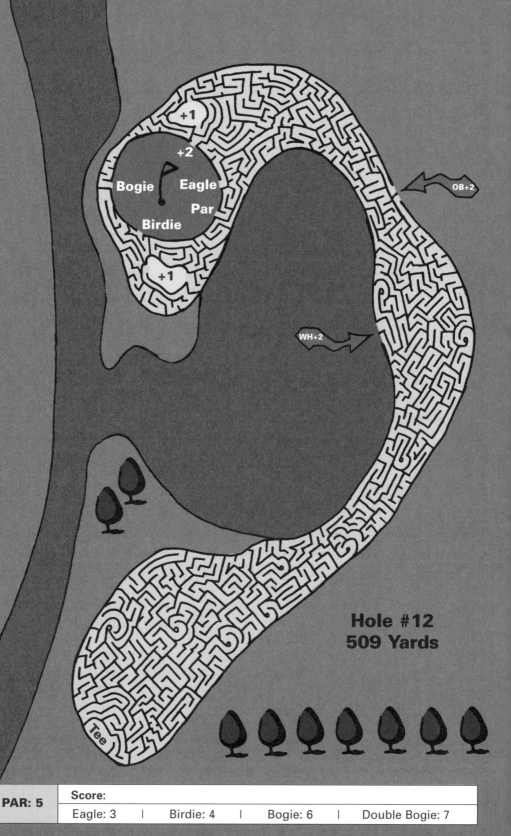

Hole #12
509 Yards

PAR: 5	Score:			
	Eagle: 3	Birdie: 4	Bogie: 6	Double Bogie: 7

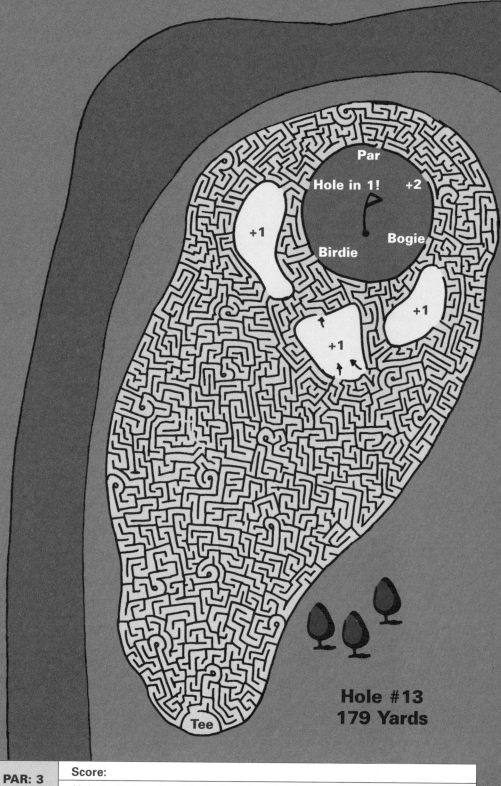

Hole #13
179 Yards

PAR: 3

Score:

Hole in 1!: 1 | Birdie: 2 | Bogie: 4 | Double Bogie: 5

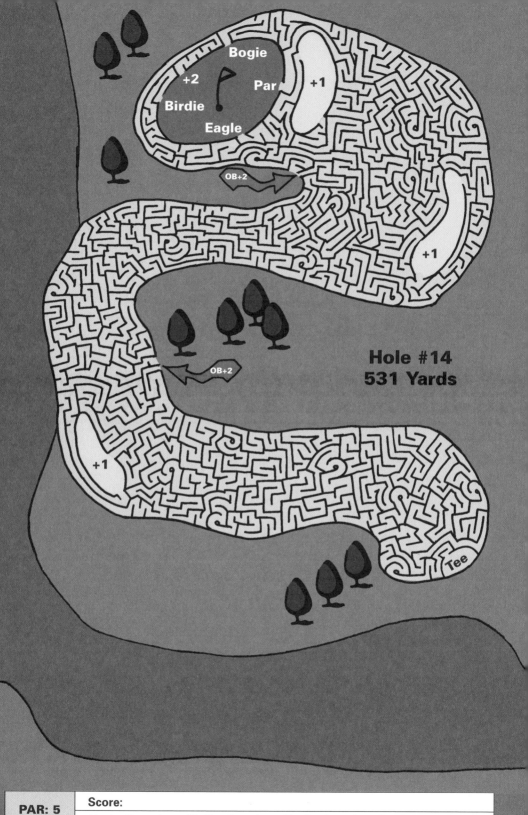

+2
Par
Bogie
Birdie
Eagle
+1
OB+2
+1

Hole #15
417 Yards

Tee

PAR: 4	Score:			
	Eagle: 2	Birdie: 3	Bogie: 5	Double Bogie: 6

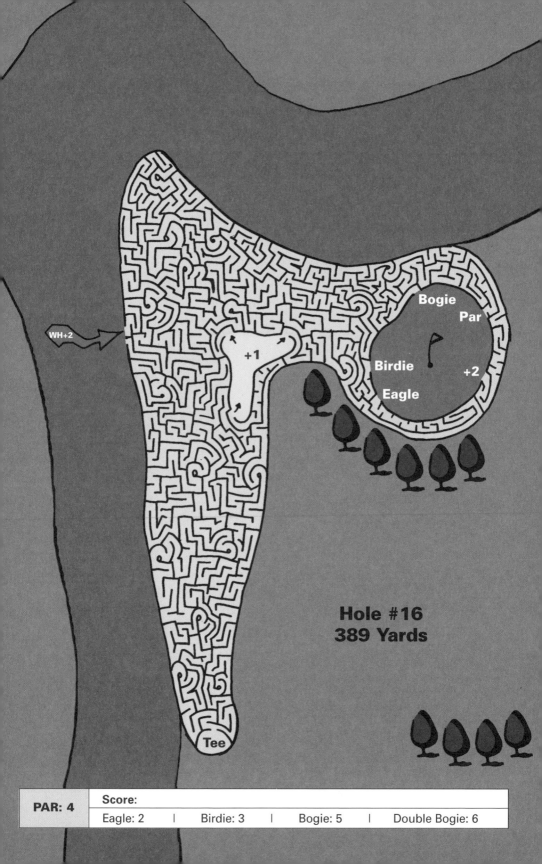

WH+2

+1

Bogie
Par

Birdie

Eagle

+2

Hole #16
389 Yards

Tee

PAR: 4	Score:			
	Eagle: 2	Birdie: 3	Bogie: 5	Double Bogie: 6

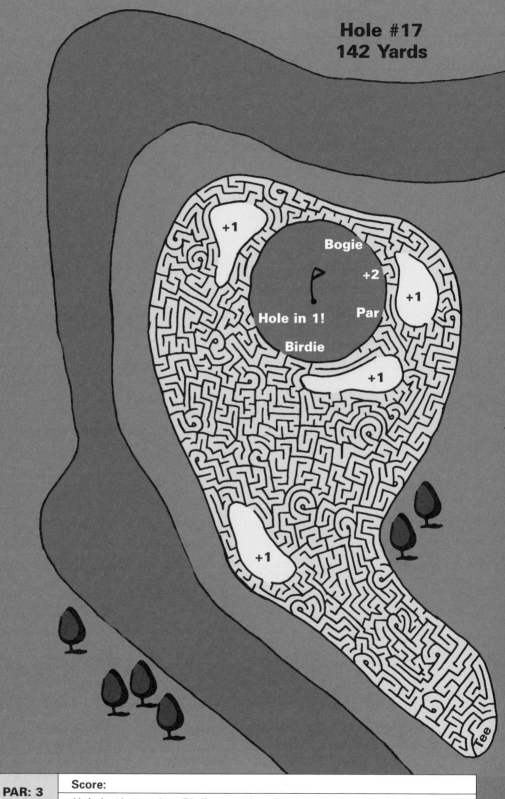

Hole #17
142 Yards

+1

Bogie

+2

Hole in 1!   Par

Birdie

+1

+1

+1

Tee

PAR: 3	Score:
	Hole in 1!: 1	Birdie: 2	Bogie: 4	Double Bogie: 5

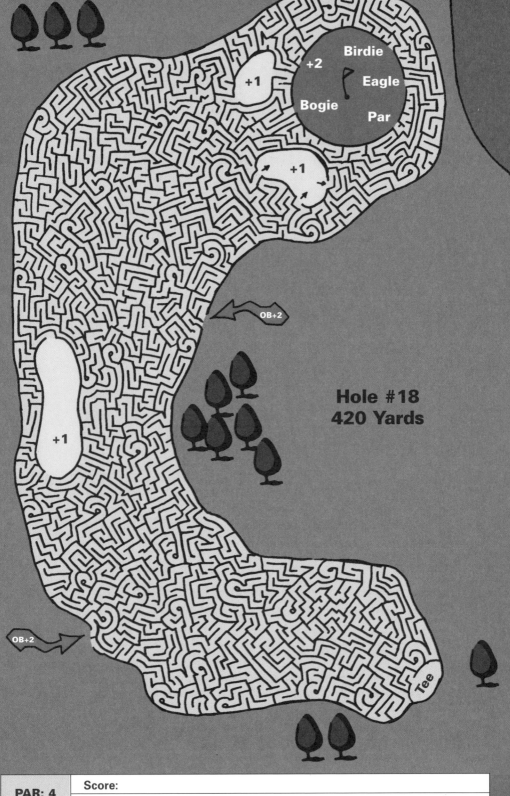

Birdie

+2

Eagle

Bogie

Par

+1

+1

OB+2

+1

Hole #18
420 Yards

OB+2

Tee

PAR: 4	Score:			
	Eagle: 2	Birdie: 3	Bogie: 5	Double Bogie: 6

SCORECARD

Maze Craze Country Club

HOLE	1	2	3	4	5	6	7	8	9	10	11	12	13	14	15	16	17	18	
YARDAGE	435	165	515	430	185	412	398	410	523	425	401	509	179	531	417	389	142	420	6889
PAR	4	3	5	4	3	4	4	4	5	4	4	5	3	5	4	4	3	4	72
PLAYER																			
2.																			

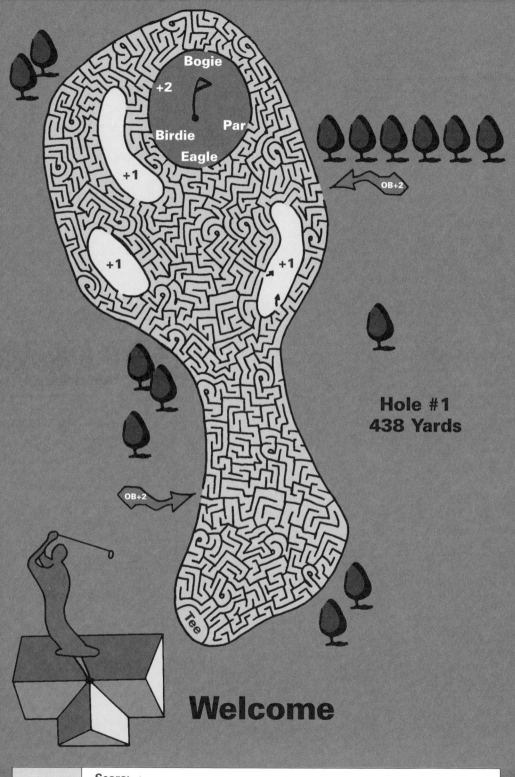

Bogie

+2

Par

Birdie

Eagle

+1

+1

+1

OB+2

Hole #1
438 Yards

OB+2

Tee

Welcome

PAR: 4	Score:			
	Eagle: 2	Birdie: 3	Bogie: 5	Double Bogie: 6

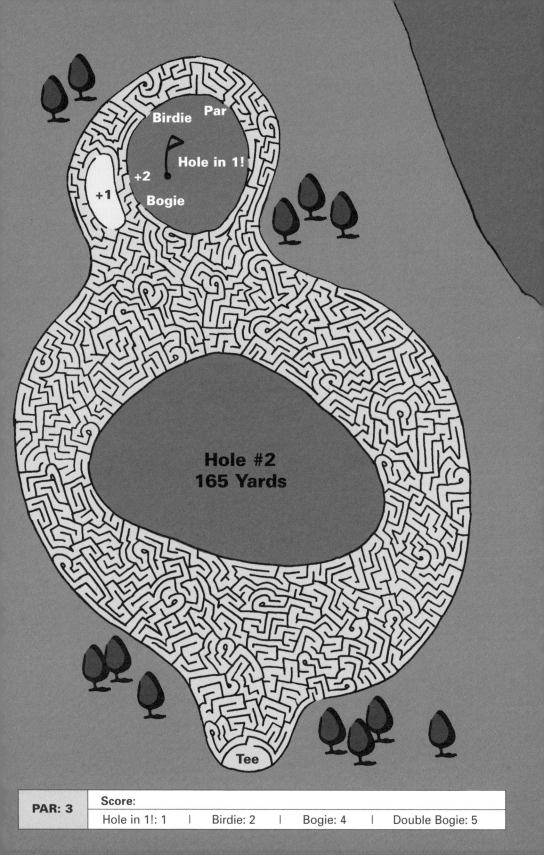

Birdie   Par

Hole in 1!

+2

+1

Bogie

Hole #2
165 Yards

Tee

PAR: 3	Score:			
	Hole in 1!: 1	Birdie: 2	Bogie: 4	Double Bogie: 5

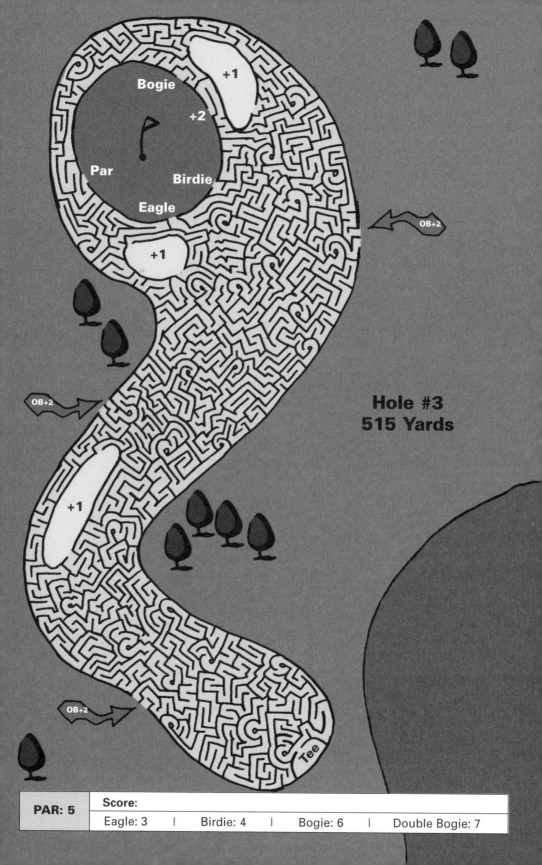

Hole #3
515 Yards

PAR: 5	Score:			
	Eagle: 3	Birdie: 4	Bogie: 6	Double Bogie: 7

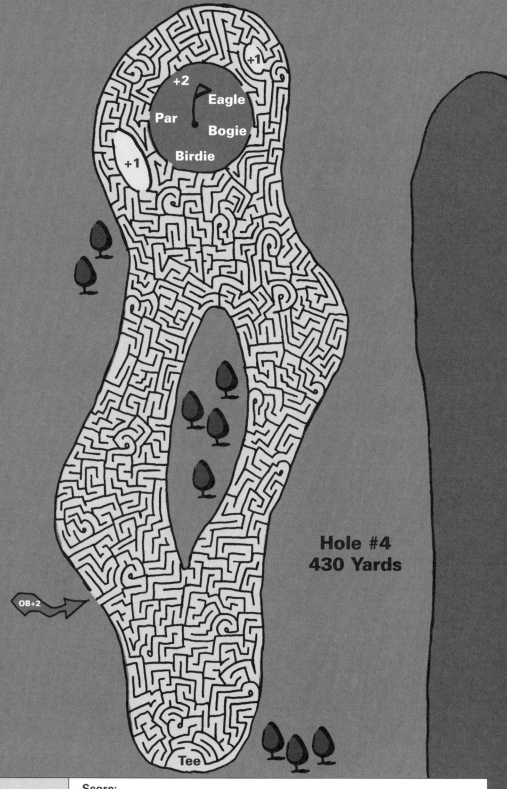

Hole #4
430 Yards

+2
Par
Eagle
Bogie
Birdie
+1
+1

OB+2

Tee

PAR: 4	Score:			
	Eagle: 2	Birdie: 3	Bogie: 5	Double Bogie: 6

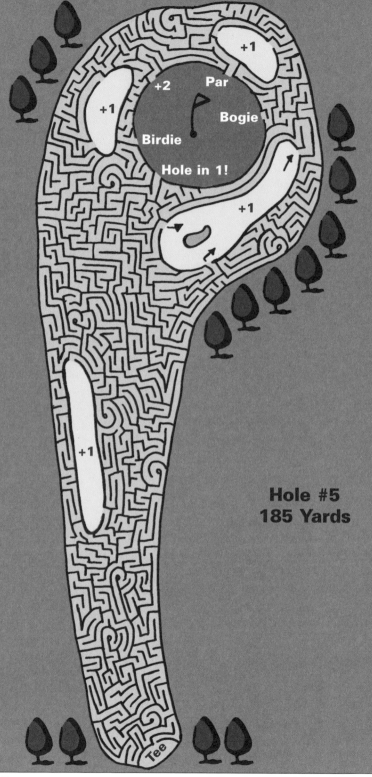

Hole #5
185 Yards

+1

+2   Par

Birdie   Bogie

Hole in 1!

+1

+1

PAR: 3	Score:			
	Hole in 1!: 1	Birdie: 2	Bogie: 4	Double Bogie: 5

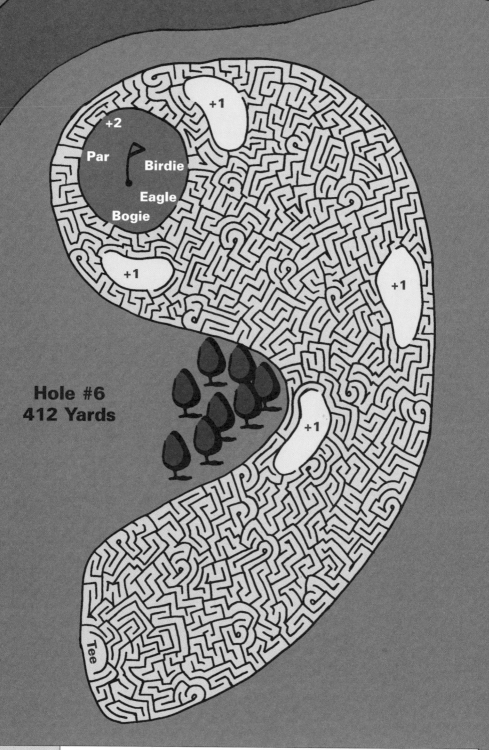

Hole #6
412 Yards

+2
Par
Birdie
Eagle
Bogie

+1

+1

+1

+1

Tee

PAR: 4	Score:			
	Eagle: 2	Birdie: 3	Bogie: 5	Double Bogie: 6

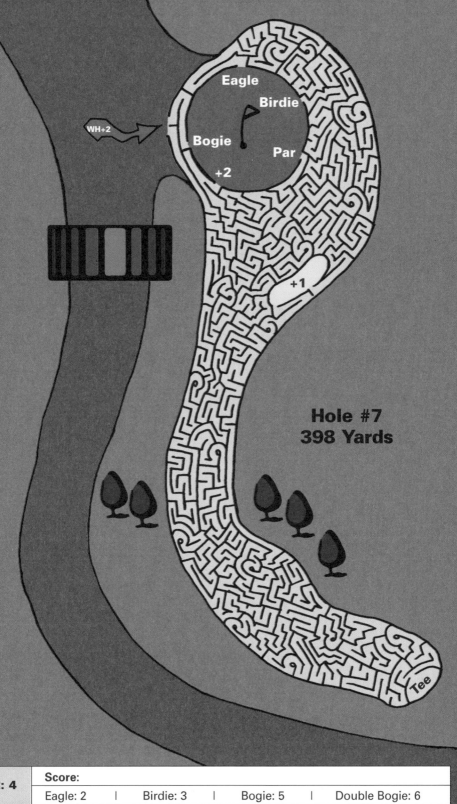

Eagle

Birdie

WH+2

Bogie

Par

+2

+1

Hole #7
398 Yards

Tee

PAR: 4	Score:			
	Eagle: 2	Birdie: 3	Bogie: 5	Double Bogie: 6

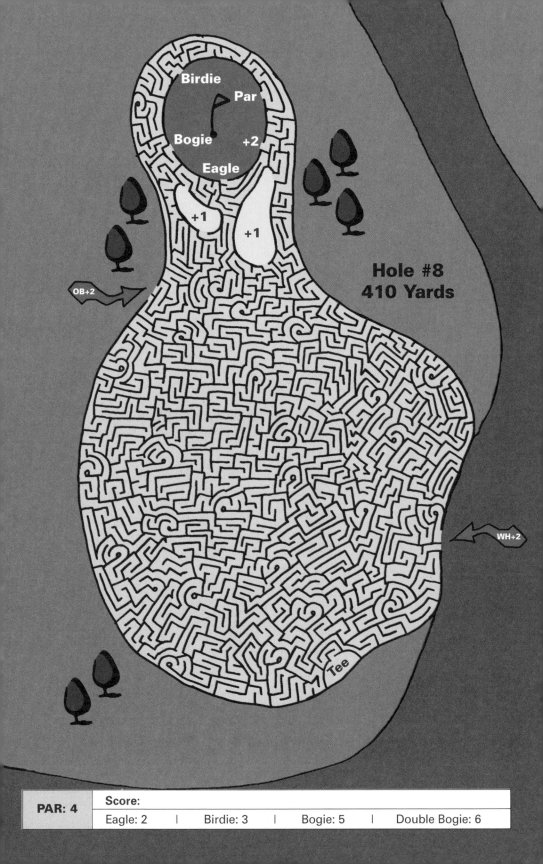

Birdie

Par

Bogie

+2

Eagle

+1

+1

OB+2

Hole #8
410 Yards

WH+2

Tee

PAR: 4	Score:			
	Eagle: 2	Birdie: 3	Bogie: 5	Double Bogie: 6

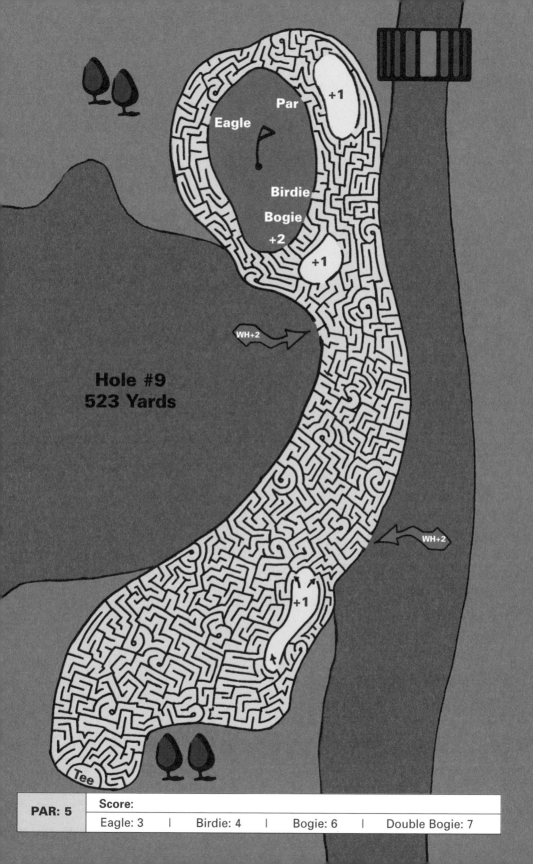

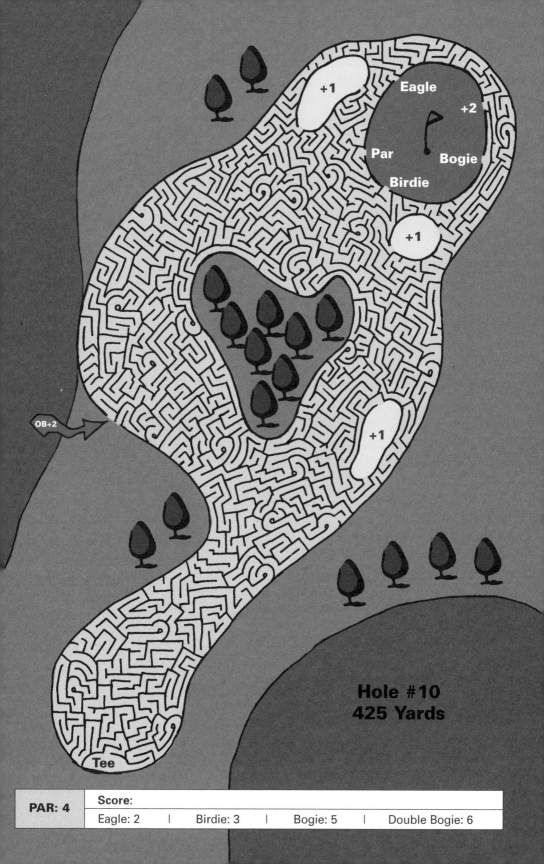

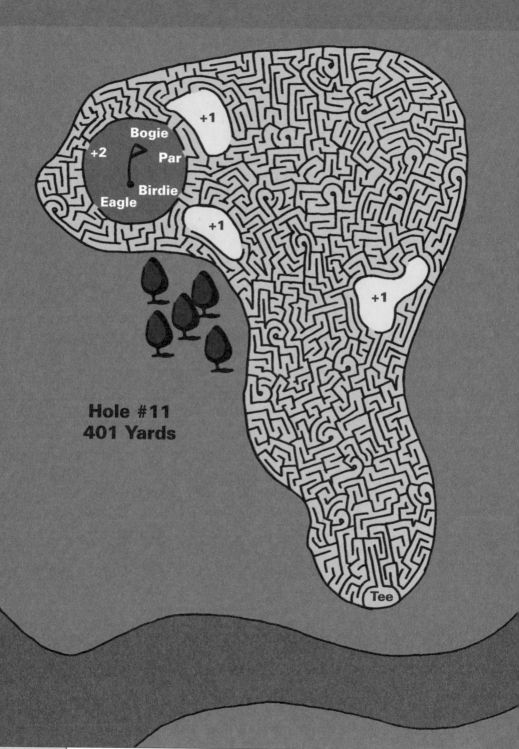

Hole #11
401 Yards

+1

+2
Bogie
Par
Birdie
Eagle

+1

+1

Tee

PAR: 4 | Score:
Eagle: 2 | Birdie: 3 | Bogie: 5 | Double Bogie: 6

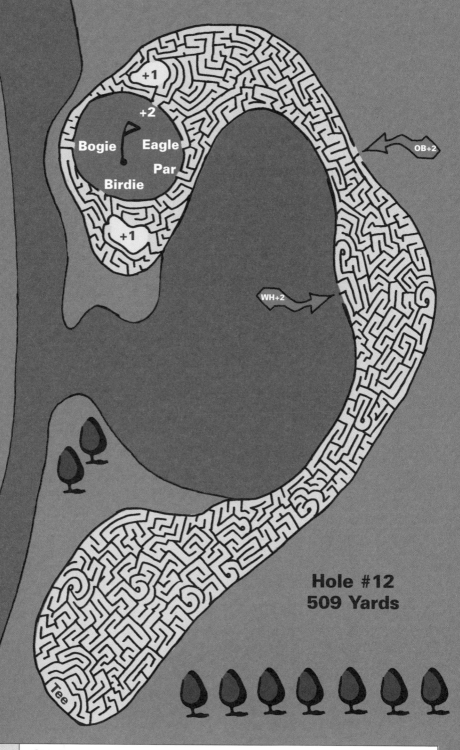

Hole #12
509 Yards

PAR: 5	Score:			
	Eagle: 3	Birdie: 4	Bogie: 6	Double Bogie: 7

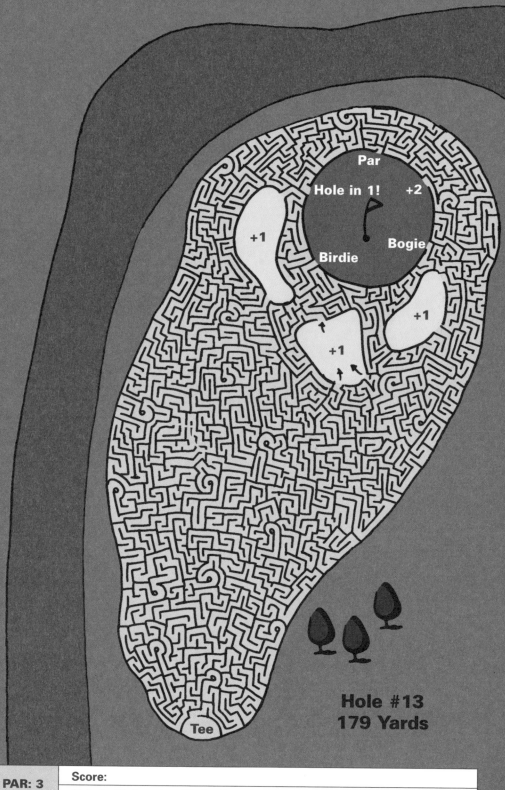

Par
Hole in 1!
+2
+1
Birdie
Bogie
+1
+1
Tee

Hole #13
179 Yards

PAR: 3

Score:

Hole in 1!: 1 | Birdie: 2 | Bogie: 4 | Double Bogie: 5

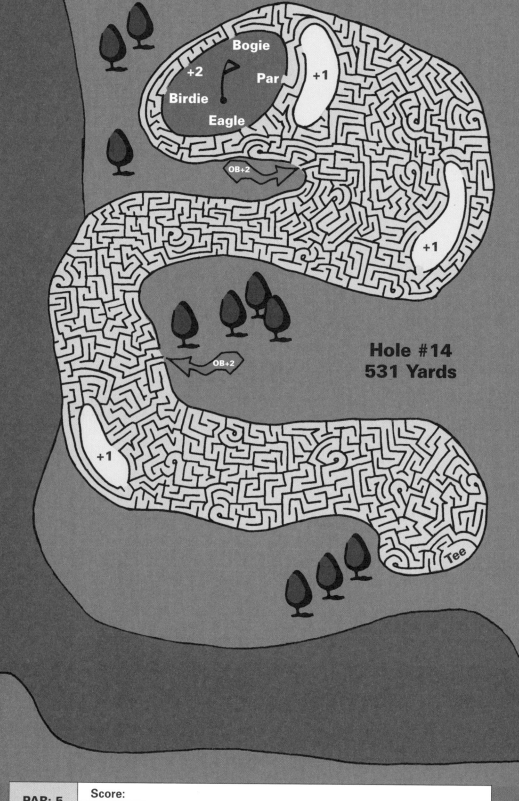

Bogie

+2

Par

+1

Birdie

Eagle

OB+2

+1

Hole #14
531 Yards

OB+2

+1

Tee

PAR: 5	Score:			
	Eagle: 3	Birdie: 4	Bogie: 6	Double Bogie: 7

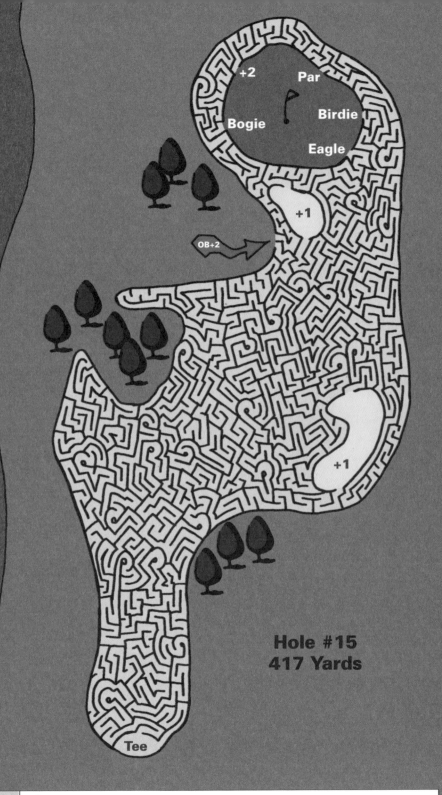

Hole #15
417 Yards

+2   Par
Bogie   Birdie
Eagle
+1
OB+2
+1
Tee

PAR: 4	Score:			
	Eagle: 2	Birdie: 3	Bogie: 5	Double Bogie: 6

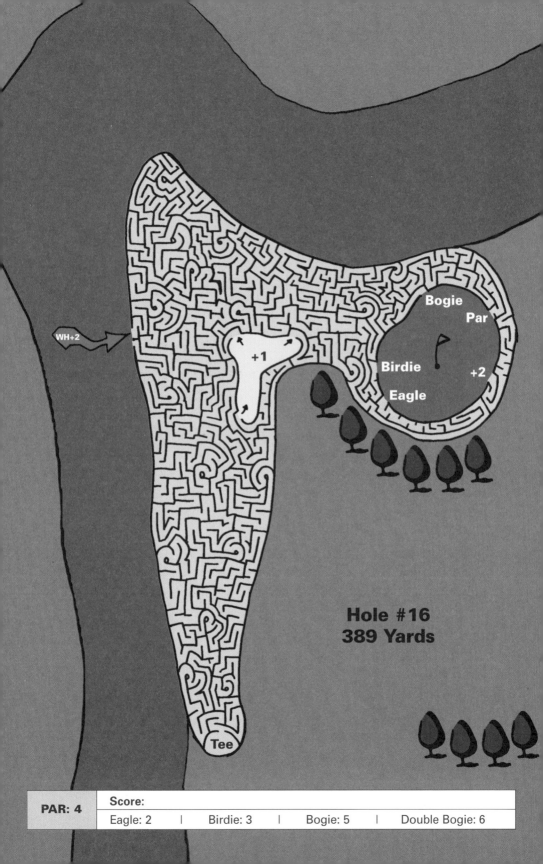

WH+2

+1

Bogie
Par
Birdie
+2
Eagle

Hole #16
389 Yards

Tee

PAR: 4	Score:			
	Eagle: 2	Birdie: 3	Bogie: 5	Double Bogie: 6

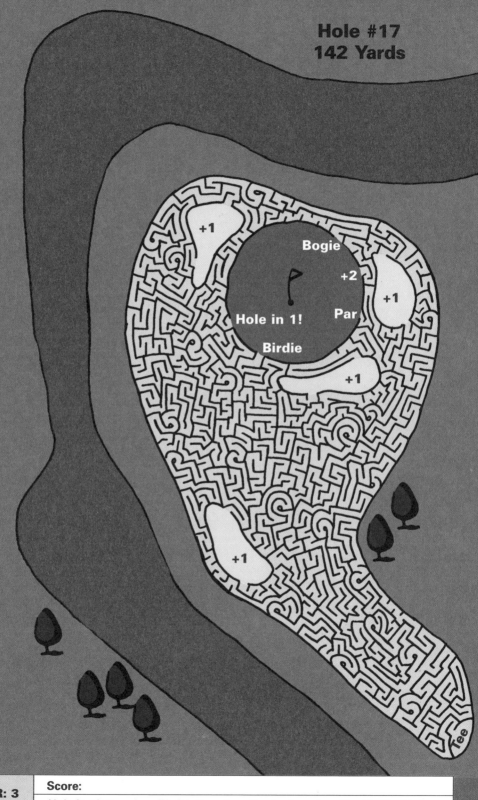

Hole #17
142 Yards

+1

Bogie

+2

+1

Hole in 1!

Par

Birdie

+1

+1

Tee

PAR: 3	Score:			
	Hole in 1!: 1	Birdie: 2	Bogie: 4	Double Bogie: 5

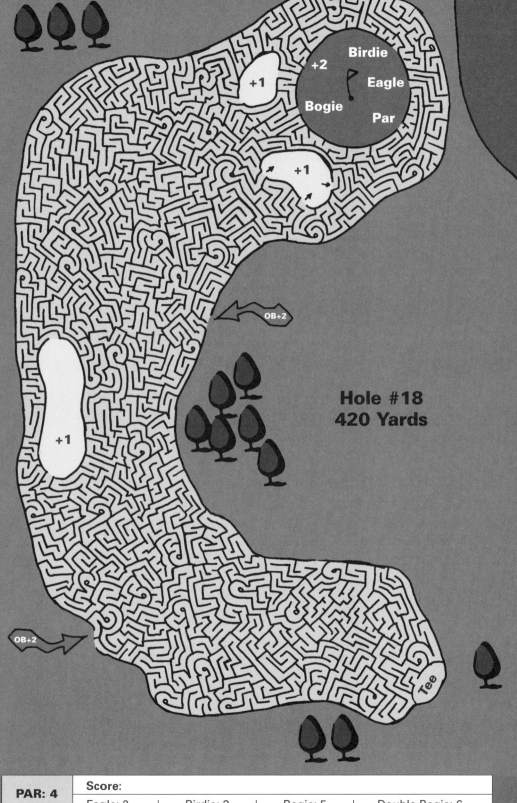

Birdie
+2
Eagle
Bogie
Par
+1
+1
OB+2
+1
Hole #18
420 Yards
OB+2
Tee

PAR: 4	Score:			
	Eagle: 2	Birdie: 3	Bogie: 5	Double Bogie: 6